Judging Handicrafts

Marmie Vergo

All rights reserved, no part of this publication may be reproduced or transmitted by any means whatsoever without the prior permission of the publisher.

Edited by Veneficia Publications
Text © Marmie Vergo
Cover image © Marmie Vergo
modified by Diane Narraway

ISBN: 978-1-914071-98-0

Veneficia Publications
June 2023

VENEFICIA PUBLICATIONS UK
veneficiapublications.com

INTRODUCTION

There are many shows needing handicraft judges but sadly there are too few handicraft judges available.

Craft work is not by any means an outdated thing. New materials, techniques and trends are continually being developed from fresh ideas. Judging needs to keep pace with what is new as well as old established craft techniques.

This book is intended as an aid to those who are proficient in some craft techniques and would like to become judges so that they can have an idea of what is expected of a craft judge. How to examine each entry; what to look for; typical flaws and suggested methods of marking.

Having been a handicraft judge as well as a lecturer and examiner in creative crafts for about fifty years I have had plenty of experience of the type and variety of crafts that are to be found on the show bench as well as that being produced by students in colleges.

There will be many entries in the classes that are easier to make, have less expensive tool requirements, or material requirements.

There will also be entries in the *'Any other item'* or *'You've made it, let's see it'* classes, which are where something has been made for which there is no specific class listed in the schedule.

There will be great diversity within this class often with unusual entries. A judge must therefore be aware of what is acceptable in all crafts exhibited to be competent to compare and judge the relative merits of the items presented in this group. This may vary between a felt needle case and a model of a Spanish galleon or model train.

The book is also intended to be an aid for those who wish to exhibit and want to improve their skills by being aware of what is expected in any craft area. It may also encourage others to try a new craft idea. Craft work is not old fashioned. It is as new as the materials used, the way in which they have been used and the ideas which create it.

It may also serve as a useful guide to those who create the classes within the schedule or the stewards who will assist the judge in a local show.

NOTE

A good judge does not need to be able to personally create all the crafts they are judging but should know the materials needed, stages of work, skills required, materials and processes used in their creation. In the same way that an art critic is not an artist, and a book critic is not a writer but both of them know what a good piece of work is.

CRAFT EXPERTISE IS REQUIRED TO COVER ALL CATEGORIES

Categories have been listed in alphabetical order.

It is worth noting that there are several *grey areas* in handicraft judging.

SUGARCRAFT

This is usually included with cookery but sometimes turns up in handicraft sections in which case it should be treated as other forms of modelling, but it is desirable for the judge to know what types of sugar recipe is required for covering the surface as opposed to that used for piping or modelling and how colour and glazed effects are created. It is also helpful to be aware of the required tools.

DRAWING AND PAINTING

These techniques are usually covered by a qualified art judge, but a situation may occur in small shows where it is not economical for a separate judge to be obtained.

Many types of media may be used such as oil, water colour, pastel, pencil, charcoal etc.

In all instances the judge needs to be able to recognise the type of media used and aware of what is good practice in the use of each.

The judge also needs to be aware of modern materials, methods and trends.

The principles of good design should be evident in each item submitted with due attention paid to the layout, proportion use of colour and skill in the use of any media.

PHOTOGRAPHY

This is another area which sometimes falls to the craft judge for reasons of economy in a small show. This has been covered in some detail as a guide should this occur as there often seems to be some difficulty in obtaining photography judges.

TYPES OF CRAFT WHICH MAY BE ENCOUNTERED

Basketry & Cane Work

Book Binding

Calligraphy

Card Making

Computer Graphics

Children's Groups

Computer graphics

Corn Dollies

Covered Boxes

Crochet – all types of traditional and Tunisian

Curtains

Cushions

Decoupage Collage and Montage

Embroidery – hand – traditional, modern, counted thread and all types of canvas work using all types of yarns.

Embroidery – machine

Fabric painting & printing

Flower Making

Glass Crafts – Painting, Engraving and Stained Glass

Glove Making

Jewellery

Knitting – hand and machine

Lace making – all varieties.

Lampshades

Leather Work

Machine Sewing Dressmaking – machine and hand.

Macrame/ Knotwork

Metalwork – joined, turned and sculpted.

Millinery

Modelling

Parchment Craft

Patchwork – all varieties

Photography – specific classifications – colour and black and white

Poker work

Pottery – thrown and moulded.

Pottery, Ceramics, Modelling and Decoration

Pressed flowers

Quilling

Quilting

Raffia Work

Rug work

Sea Grass Seat Weaving

Smocking

Soft toy making – knitted, pieced, rag and composite.

Spinning

Tailoring – full and soft

Tatting

Upholstery

Weaving – loom, braid and card

Woodwork & wood carving – joined, turned and carved.

WHAT TO LOOK FOR

IN

EACH CRAFT

BASKETRY AND CANE WORK

- Canes used for spokes and randing should be of suitable thickness for their purpose and suitably prepared together with any bases before commencement of work.

- The base should have been worked with suitable materials using methods appropriate for the design.

- Spokes should have been correctly and evenly kinked according to design and the spoke spread should be even in similar areas of a design.

- Upright stakes should have been inserted to a suitable depth.

- The turning point of the base and the upright should be suitably strengthened with some form of upsetting.

- Upright work should be evenly shaped.

- Randing should be even throughout the work.

- Any handles should be suitably and firmly attached and wrapped.

- Top edges should be suitably beaded and bordered as appropriate.

- Wooden bases should have been drilled with even sized holes evenly spaced around the edge and smoothed before use.

- Wooden based items should have a foot trac of a suitable depth with a row or rows of waling and / or upsetting before randing is done.

- Framed cane or basket work should have been finished with neat beading and wrapping (with split cane) or plait border on the upper edge with scalloming on any corners.

- All canes should have been neatly and evenly cut on the inside of the work.

BOOK BINDING

- Cover materials are suitable for type of book.

- Signatures are neatly sewn & knotted.

- Not too many pages per signature.

- Signatures are correctly joined together.

- Text block pages neatly trimmed.

- Cover boards are the same size.

- Boards are sharply cut with separate spine.

- Boards are correctly covered.

- Spine is reinforced.

- Boards are marginally larger than the text block.

- Correct type of end paper chosen.

- End papers neatly cut and attached.

- No air bubbles visible behind end papers.

- Finished book surfaces should be very flat and smooth.

- All corners should be neat.

CALLIGRAPHY

GENERAL

- The same type of script should have been used throughout.

- The same width of writing tool should have been used throughout except for illuminated capital letters.

- All lines of writing should be horizontal across the page and parallel with one another.

- All lines of script should be an appropriate and even distance apart.

- There should be no blots or ink spatters and no remaining evidence of erasure.

- The work should be clean, with surfaces smooth and flat and appropriately presented.

- The finished effect should be uniform and pleasing to view.

- Most of the above points will be sufficient to determine superiority.

TECHNICAL SPECIFICATIONS.

- Italic script should be oval in form and not round; Gothic / Old English script should be rectangular and narrow or square in form and Carolingian script should be round.

- Spacing between words should equate to width of small letter "o" in the type of script being used and not wider.

- Italic script – small letters should be 5 nib widths in height, with ascenders / descenders 9 – 9.5 pen widths (4 more than small letters), approximately double.

- Gothic / Old English script – small letters should be about 5 pen widths high (ascenders 2 higher and descenders 3 lower). The space between letters should be about one pen width. Capitals are the same height as ascenders and round in form.

- In all scripts, the spacing between rows should allow the same space or one pen width more than the space taken up by ascenders and descenders of consecutive rows.

- Old English and Gothic scripts are upright (pen 45') with letters joined by an upstroke at the top of the first down stroke of the next letter. Ascenders and round topped letters are not joined. Any ascenders with cross strokes – "f's" and "t's" etc. – should have the cross – stroke level with the top of the small letters.

- Italic script – letters should slope a little towards the right – same angle throughout. Within a word, letters should join to form a cursive script – breaks before letters "b," "f," "h," "k," "l," and "t" only. Letters are joined from the bottom to the top of the next by a hairline upstroke. The exceptions being the letters "f," "t," "v," "w," and "x" which join from the top to the next letter and "e," which joins from the mid – section to the next letter when the starting point of the next letter is at the top. Capitals should be 7 nib widths high or match ascenders.

CARD MAKING

- The design should be suitable for the card stock chosen.

- All edges should be smoothly cut.

- Card should be sharply folded.

- Inserts should be minimally glued to centre of folded card.

- Inserts should not show from outside of card and inserts should be lighter in weight than main card.

- Attachments to card should be neatly and smoothly glued or firmly fixed.

- Spacers should not be visible from the front on decoupage.

- Attachment edges should be smoothly cut without blebs.

- Deckle and scalloped edges should be cut so that pattern is continuous.

- Attachments should be evenly placed.

- Any embossing should be evenly and smoothly worked.

- Pinholes should be evenly spaced and close enough for a lace effect.

- Colour application should be carefully done to create a pleasing design.

- Lettering should be smooth and even throughout and should be compatible with design features.

- Ribbons or cords should be neatly tied and attached, and sequins, stones and other findings should not fall off when handled.

CHILDREN'S GROUPS

- The aim in judging these groups is primarily to encourage more entries and produce society members of the future.

- The most popular classes of children's entries are things such as edible necklaces; animals made from fruit and vegetables; decorated paper plates; decorated eggs; drawings or posters; cardboard, or paper models and some forms of simple embroidery.

- It is preferable to be judging small age bands within any one class, particularly with younger age groups as manipulative ability is not as well developed as in older children.

- Ideally "6 and under", "7 – 11" and "12 – 16 "year groupings as comparison of abilities with small age gaps is easier.

- Be aware of average abilities within each age range so that exceptional skill is then obvious.

- Reward imaginative skill as well as manipulative skill.

- Decide between care of presentation of the mundane versus imaginative work with a few blemishes.

- Be aware of what is obviously adult assisted.

- Give plenty of commendations.

COMPUTER GRAPHICS

Types of computer graphics that may be presented:

- Typewritten images

- Regular tool shapes which may be pattern or colour filled

- Free hand shapes drawn with brush or pencil tool which may be pattern or colour filled.

- Clip art shapes – pre – coloured, user coloured or uncoloured

- Scanned images.

- Digital photographic images

- All of the above may be with or without added text in picture, leaflet, greetings card, brochure or poster form. In all cases the degree of skill required in producing a pleasing design / layout should be taken into consideration during assessment.

ASSESSMENT

- The layout and presentation of the whole should be pleasing and of well - balanced composition and proportion.

- Colour schemes should enhance the effect of the graphics with gradient and radiant fills showing more skill than single colour or tab pattern fills.

- All lines and shapes whether tool bar or free hand should be well drawn and effective.

- Clip art should be well placed (and appropriately filled if necessary) in relation to the rest of the design.

- Scanned images should be aligned vertically with the page.

- Scanning and digital images should be at a suitable resolution to produce a good, printed image, particularly if presented in photographic form.

- Touch up work should blend smoothly with the rest of the image using suitable tools (e.g., cloning tool).

- Freeform cutting and pasting should have been done with neat outlines without any unwanted background excess remaining and should blend into background into which it is placed.

- Borders where used should be of a suitable width and composition to enhance the presentation.

- Text should be done with fonts of an appropriate style, size and colour for the graphic design with word extrusions or wrappings following a smooth shape or path.

- Printing should have been done on a paper suitable to the type of graphic presented.

CORN DOLLIES

- Straw used should be in good condition (preferably of the hollow type), have been suitably prepared and evenly graded throughout the piece of work.

- Starting and finishing ends should have been neatly and firmly tied using suitable yarn.

- Braiding or plaiting should be evenly done.

- Joining should be done on the corners by well – fitting insertions.

- Kinking should be at even distances apart on each round and shapes smoothly tapered to give good outlines.

COVERED BOXES

- The material to be covered should be firm enough for the project chosen.

- Shapes should be matching and smoothly cut with sharp corners.

- Material chosen for covering the shapes should be appropriate for the project.

- Any glue used should not have 'bled' through the covering material.

- Glued paper or other unwoven covering should not show any bubbling in the glued areas.

- Any seaming should be in line with the edges of the shape.

- Any edge stitching should be inconspicuous.

- Linings should be neatly attached and not visible from the outside.

- The covering should be tautly fixed to the box shape.

CROCHET

- Hook size suitable for yarn size

- Even stitchery and tension

- All ends sewn off.

- Joins made at the ends of a row or by splicing.

- No knots

- Suitable method of seaming and assembly.

- Textured stitches only lightly pressed.

- Lace items blocked to a regular shape.

- Outer edge stitches should be blocked to an even shape.

- Three dimensional items suitably stiffened to hold shape.

CURTAINS

- Patterns should be matched when hanging in pairs.

- Heading tape should be compatible with curtain fabric weight.

- Side turnings should be correctly fitted to linings.

- Linings and curtain hem stitching should not be visible.

- All corners should be mitred.

- Heading tapes should be neatly and accurately applied.

- Provision to be made for tape cord.

- Pairs of curtains should be the same length.

- All seaming should be well pressed.

CUSHIONS

- The cushion should be well shaped with suitable fabrics chosen for end use.

- Fillings should be of suitable materials and should be evenly distributed inside a fabric bag (filling pad)

- For washable covers there should be an opening to insert filling pad with suitable method of fastening

- The cushion pad should fill the cover & maintain shape.

- Any piping or cording around the edge should have been neatly joined.

- Frills should have been evenly placed with no tightness on corners.

- Any decoration should have been appropriately worked and finished.

- Any borders should be of an even width.

- The inside of a removable cover should be neatly finished.

DECOUPAGE, COLLAGE, AND MONTAGE

These all involve cutting out shapes and applying them to another surface to form a type of decoration. Cutting outlines should be smooth with glue applied evenly to give a smooth surface and of a pleasing design.

COLLAGE

This is usually a collection of paper pictures, cut out and stuck to another surface, usually paper such as in a scrap book to form a decorative effect. Pattern or picture.

- There should be an obvious theme to the collection.

- The background material and surface should be appropriate for the items to be affixed to it.

- Any gluing or other fixing should have been firmly, neatly and unobtrusively done.

- Where paper items are included, they may be cut, torn or folded as appropriate to the design and theme.

- Overlapping of images is permitted but the surface should not become lumpy because of this.

DECOUPAGE

This is similar with paper cut – outs but usually stuck to a hard surface such as small table surfaces, screens or boxes. The decorative area is then varnished to make the surface of the item durable.

This may also be a collection of identical images applied one on top of the other, with small spacers between, to give a three – dimensional effect.

The images may be identical in colour or shades, according to the design.

The spacers should not be visible from the front and should be of an even thickness with the pictures smoothly edged and glue carefully applied.

Usually no more than three layers are applied.

- The hard surface used should be suitably prepared for the design chosen.

- Surfaces are usually smooth.

- The collection of images used should have been glued to the smooth surface so that no glue residue is visible.

- There should be no bubbling of the glue which would make the surface of the finished application uneven.

- The applied materials should form a pleasing effect.

- The design should have been varnished to protect and preserve it. Several thin coats of varnish are preferable to one thick one.

- This may also be a collection identical images applied one on top of the other with small spacers between to give a three – dimensional effect.

- The images should be of identical objects and the same size.

- The images may be identical in colour or shades, according to the design.

- The spacers should not be visible from the front.

- The spacers should be an even thickness.

- The edges of the pictures should be smoothly cut with no blebs.

- Glue must be carefully applied with no overruns.

- Usually no more than three layers are applied.

MONTAGE

A similar effect to collage, but using a variety of paper, fabric yarn and any other suitable materials to form a pleasing picture or presentation of ideas. It may be a crafts person's storyboard showing ideas, shapes, colours and materials. It may also be a series of items or pictures leading to the formation of other ideas.

- The items included should give enough information to a crafts person for them to be able to understand the creation of the ideas being presented in a storyboard type of montage.

- The items may also be indicative of a progression of ideas, which should be obvious.

- The mounting base material should be appropriate and firm enough to support the materials and items used.

- The theme of what is being presented should be apparent.

- All materials should be firmly fixed. The fixing materials should be appropriate to the material being fixed. Some items may be only partially fixed.

- Many different types of materials may form part of a montage.

- The diversity of materials and shapes and colour schemes will be taken into consideration as will their suitability to the design.

- The finished item should be neat and pleasing to look at.

EMBROIDERY

SURFACE DECORATION USING A FORM OF STITCHERY:

- The fabrics / yarns chosen should be suitable for the design.

- Fabrics and yarns should be suitable for the end use.

- The use of colour should be pleasing.

- Combinations of stitches chosen should be appropriate for fabric, end use and enhance the design.

- The techniques chosen should be suitable for the design.

- Technique chosen should be suitable for the end use.

- Yarn thickness should be appropriate for the design and fabric.

- Embellishments should be compatible with design, materials, and end use.

- Any guide /design outlines should have been removed or covered.

- Precautions should have been taken to keep work flat and unwrinkled.

- Support fabric should have been used for machine embroidery.

- Support fabric should have been removed/ hidden after work.

- Hand embroidery should be neat on the reverse.

- Canvas work should be done using yarn appropriate to fabric thread count.

- All over designs should have no missed stitches and be done using the same direction of stitch throughout.

- Ends should be neatly sewn off on the wrong side – no knots to cause an uneven surface visible on the right side.

FABRIC PAINTING & PRINTING

Type of paint or mixture of colouring media which may have been used will probably be from the following readily available list:

- Silk paint – Either using gutta or without using gutta.

- Using salt crystals, light reactive effects

- Acrylic fabric paints or crafter's acrylic used with extender.

- Fabric felt pens.

- Plastic paints

- Melted wax pigments.

- Fabric inks

- Fabric dyes

- Metallic or pearl or opalescent finish and opalescent additives.

- Fabric glue with applied metal foil coating.

- Heat expanding paints.

- Iron on computer graphic printed transfers.

Methods of application of colour will be from the following:

- Freehand

- Stencil

- Block print

- Roller print

- Screen print

- Batik or other resist process

- Tie dye

- Heat transfer

ASSESSMENT

- There should be no remaining evidence of any guidelines used for marking the design.

- The type of paint used should be compatible with the end use.

- The type of fibre content should be suitable to the colour and consistency of the medium used.

- The fabric weave should be suitable for the application of the colour and consistency of the medium used.

- Outlines of colour should be clean and not smudged.

- Where gutta, resist wax or other outlining media are used they should be of a uniform width throughout.

- There should be no evidence of unintentional colour bleeding (except in batik).

- Surface applications of background colour should be even in graduations of density.

- Single uniform coloration should not show evidence of having been allowed to dry during application.

- Colour media should be of the correct consistency for the type of work.

- All work should have been well pressed or steamed to fix colours.

- Computer transfers should not have excessive border edges and should not show tears in design caused by transfer removal after heat setting.

- Appreciation should be given to the complexity of design / type of work.

- Overall effect should be pleasing.

- Presentation of work should be appropriate.

- Standard of workmanship should be high.

FLOWER MAKING

- Materials used should be appropriate for the type of flora being made.

- Techniques for assembly will depend on end use.

- Silk flowers may be created using purchased stamens if desired.

- Petals made from fantasy film or dipped other plastic should have a fine wire edge which is strong enough to hold the shape of the petal. This would generally mean the larger the petal the thicker the wire needed.'

- Raw edged fabric petals should have no evidence of unintentional fraying.

- Some suitable form of stiffening may be desirable.

- Stems should be of a suitable thickness of wire and firmly attached to the flower head.

- Stems should be covered with suitable binding materials and of plausible or acceptable colouring.

- Realistic flowers should include a calyx.

- Realistic or stylised leaves should be included in any arrangement.

- Paper flowers should have parts firmly fixed using suitable glue of other methods to form stable flower heads.

- Fresh flower arranging materials may be used to assist in creating a stable display.

- Any corsage should have some form of fastening.

- Finished flowers should be arranged to best advantage.

- Warning – very fine fabrics may wilt in damp conditions.

GLASS CRAFTS

Suitable artefacts should be chosen for type of glass decoration.

- Suitable paints/tools should be chosen compatible with end use.

- Designs should be pleasing but not too complex according to type of work.

PAINTING ON GLASS

- Outliners should have been evenly and smoothly applied.

- There should be no bleeding in filling colours.

- The painting should have been fixed to make it permanent.

ENGRAVING ON GLASS

• Shapes should be clearly incised or outlined.

• Design outlines should have been removed or hidden.

• Glass should be well polished after completion.

STAINED GLASS

• Design should be suitable for the type of glass used. Shapes should be cut smoothly and evenly.

• No false cuts or scratched areas should be visible.

• Soldering should have been smoothly applied with no gaps.

• Soldering should have been of an even width throughout.

GLOVE MAKING

- Leather or fabric chosen should be suitable for the craft, having been suitably prepared.

- Tranks, fourchettes, thumbs and quirks (where used) should have been smoothly cut to the correct size to fit to each other neatly.

- Seaming allowance should be appropriate to the materials used.

- Yarn used for sewing should be compatible to fabric structure and of a suitable gauge.

- Sewing stitches should be neat and even.

- Any points should have been worked in the correct direction.

- The thumb should have been correctly inserted on the palm side of the glove and firmly sewn so that there are no gaps in the stitching during use.

- The ends of the fingers should be neatly finished and not bulky.

- Lining (where used) should have been attached inside at the ends of the fingers and under the lower edge of the trank which should be neatly sewn or smoothly cut / shaped.

- Mittens may be presented with either a gusseted thumb or a grown – on thumb.

- The backs and palms of mittens may be made from differing materials.

JEWELLERY

- Materials used are suitable for the design.

- Clasps used are of a suitable weight/ size.

- Strings or thongs should be of a suitable diameter / weight.

- Clasps are firmly fixed to strings/ thongs.

- Any jump rings used are firmly and evenly closed.

- Neat soldering of jump rings is desirable.

- Beads should not have been threaded too tightly or too loosely.

- Coils in wire should be smooth with ends turned in.

- Head pin loops should be central.

- All wire ends should be neatly and safely finished.

- Any wire wrapped items should be secure in their setting.

- Lamp work beads should have spindles completely filled.

- Lamp work beads should be well shaped.

- Peyote stitch items should have beads evenly spaced.

- Cabochons and other stones should be firmly fixed.

- Enamelling should be done on a suitable metal base.

- Outlining should be fine and even with colours neatly applied.

- Edges should be smoothed before firing and polished afterwards.

KNITTING

HAND KNITTING

- Even stitches – no stretched stitches.

- Good even tension

- Good raised textured stitches

- Textured stitches should not show mistakes.

- Even ribbing done on smaller size needles.

- Left and right fronts of garments should have the same number of rows.

- Joins in yarn should have been made at the end of a row or yarn spliced.

- No knots should be evident on the inside of garment.

- Smooth seaming – as flat as possible.

- Seaming stitches should be even and not show gaps.

- Seams should have been lightly pressed.

- Armhole seaming should be neat and smooth.

- Sleeves wide enough / not too tight

- Buttons sewn on with knitting yarn and not sewing yarn.

- Ensure that the buttonholes are the right size for the buttons.

- Check for variations in the dye lots.

- All ends should have been sewn in.

MACHINE KNITTING

- Ribbing machine cast – on should not be too loose.

- Ribs done by hand or machine should use suitable size needles.

- Tension compatible with yarn size.

- Joins made at seam edges.

- No knots visible.

- Bound off edges should not have any missed stitches.

- Intarsia work should not have long floats on the reverse.

- Floats more than about 5 stitches should have been sewn in.

- All intarsia ends should have been sewn in.

- Colour changes should not show gaps.

- Seaming done by linker should show no gaps.

- Seaming done by hand should be even.

- On a straight seam the linking should be in the same wale or row.

- Check for gaps in linked seaming – missed stitches in the chain.

- Twisted stitches should be evenly spaced.

LACE

- This may be any method of twisting or knotting yarn to form a pattern.

- Type of yarn should be suitable for type of work.

- Pattern should be evident throughout the work.

- Tension should be even throughout.

- Similar stitches should be even throughout the piece.

- The materials chosen should be compatible with the end use.

- All ends should have been neatly sewn off.

- Both sides of the work should be neatly finished

- Finished articles should have been blocked to regular shapes.

- If lace is attached to an item, joining method should be appropriate.

LAMPSHADES

- Frames should be bound and neatly finished for covered frames.to form a firm basis for stitching. Matching binding may be used.

- Fabric covered frames should show minimum evidence of stitchery with any seaming attached to struts of frame.

- Attention should be paid to the grain of the fabric so that there are no wrinkles or bulges in the cover, and it fits closely to the frame.

- Balloon linings should be bias cut and fixed so as not to show from the outside.

- Braiding and fringing should be neatly and evenly hand attached to the bottom or top struts of the frame.

- Knotwork covers should have all ends neatly fastened.

LEATHER WORK

GENERAL

The type and thickness of the leather should be suitable for the type of work.

TOOLED, PUNCHED, & EMBOSSED LEATHER

- The leather chosen should be thick enough to take a reasonable depth of impression.

- The clarity of the design should show that the leather was suitably prepared prior to use.

- Tooling should have been evenly done with precision so that the design is crisp with holes and slots having clean outlines.

- There should be no snags in cutting or other evidence of over tooling.

- Straight edges should have been knife cut with no blebs.

- Staining should have been applied evenly.

- Extra colouring should have been done with suitable durable media.

- The length of any visible cut edges should be wax finished.

- The finished item should have been suitably polished and presented.

STITCHED LEATHER WORK

- The article made should have been cut from unblemished parts of the skin and be of a uniform thickness.

- A suitable stitch length, method of stitching and type of thread should have been chosen according to the thickness of the leather and end use.

- There should be no bunching of stitches caused by the leather sticking when passing under the foot of a machine. A leather or roller foot should have been used.

- A leather needle should have been used to cleanly pierce the leather and not cause unnecessary stretching or distortion.

- Suitable support materials should have been used where required.

- Pressing should have been done either with a cool iron or a suitable weight press.

- Impression marks should not be evident on the right side.

- Top stitching should have been done with evenly spaced stitches.

- Thinning, skiving, or hammering should have been done on seaming to reduce bulk.

- Any buttonholes, eyelet holes or other incisions should have been evenly formed and suitably finished to give strength and prevent tearing or weakness in wear.

- Any decorative stitching or thonging should have been neatly worked with even spacing and a uniform thickness of decorative material.

- Any adhesive used to produce a flat or secure finish should be compatible to the leather, not visible during use and not be subject to degradation or discoloration of the surface of the fabric. The completed item should have all edges suitably finished, all surfaces suitably smoothed and should be of a pleasing appearance and fit for its purpose.

- Leather used for garments will have required pressing. Check that this has caused no surface damage – iron marks, shiny patches etc.

MACHINE SEWING

- The garment / item should be well balanced.

- Fabric should be suitable for the item.

- Interlining or support materials should be used in collar, neck, pocket and cuff areas of garments and any other areas needing extra strength such as buttonholes.

- Cutting should be done to match patterns on fabrics.

- Grain direction should be the same throughout the item, except for decorative pattern effects using stripes or similar.

- Seaming should be smooth.

- Machine tension should be correctly adjusted.

- Some form of seam finish should be evident in fraying fabrics.

- Appropriate seaming should be used throughout.

- Similar seaming should be used throughout.

- Turnings should be trimmed or otherwise finished to an even width.

- Dart shaping should have smooth points.

- Seams and darts should be adequately pressed.

- Hems should be evenly turned and appropriately sewn.

- Seam, hem, and dart impressions should not be visible on the right side of the article.

- Gathers / pleats should have been evenly worked and pressed.

- Suitable openings should have been provided.

- Fastenings should be appropriate, large enough and correctly worked.

MACRAME / KNOTWORK

• Thickness of yarn should be appropriate for the end use.

• Type of yarn should depend on whether the item is to be used indoors or outside and needs to be weather resistant or to be appropriately treated either before or after construction.

• Consideration should also be given to any cleaning which may be required.

• The design and type of knots used should be appropriate for the end use.

• There should be no joins in the lengths of yarn. The lengths should have been calculated and cut to allow for this.

• Knotting should be done evenly with the size determined by the ply and weight of the yarn.

- Fringes or fringed ends should be done using simple overhand knots, windings or decorated knots such as a Turks Head

- Provision should be made for displaying the item to best advantage especially for hanging items such as plant holders, curtains, net containers etc.

METALWORK

- The composition and gauge of the metal should be appropriate to the task.

- All cut sheet edges should have been smoothed to reduce sharpness.

- Formed shapes should be smooth and even in outline with no distortion of the metal.

- The methods of joining should be suitable for the materials and type/area of design.

- Joined sections should have been soldered, welded, brazed, screwed, riveted or bolted according to the material, use and stress loading of that area of the design.

- Joint sections should be smooth and fit well.

- There should be no evidence of surplus joining materials on the right side – these should be minimised during surface finishing.

TURNED

- Turned items should show no evidence of tool marks.

- Turned items should have well defined smooth outlines with no ridges showing unevenness of pressure on tools.

- Jaw and face plate markings should have been removed with a finish equivalent to the rest of the work.

- Any brazed, soldered, riveted screwed or bolted additions should have the joints suitably smoothed / polished /finished.

HAMMERED OR INCISED WORK

- The choice of material should be appropriate to this type of work.

- The thickness of the material should be appropriate to the type of work / design of the item.

- Un – hammered or incised areas should be smooth and free from distortion.

- Patterned areas should show even patterning.

- Similar areas of patterning should show an even degree of indentation.

- Tool marks should not be visible on the right side of the work.

- Polishing or other distress type finish should be evidenced on the right side of the work. The finished item should be stable.

MILLINERY

This heading covers all forms of head wear, but for this classification will be deemed to only cover blocked and stitched hats as knitted types will be covered by knitting techniques.

GENERAL

- The hat should be well shaped with smooth outlines.

- The materials and methods of construction should be suitable for the design.

- The choice of any embellishment should enhance rather than overpower the hat.

- Construction should be sound and sequentially correct to produce the best effect.

- There should be no unsightly stitching, raw edges or ends visible on the outside.

- Support materials should have been used where required and suitably applied.

- Some method of stabilising the head size should have been used.

- Any lining materials whether loose or fitted should have been appropriately inserted.

- Work should be clean and well presented.

TECHNICAL – BLOCKED HATS

- Blocked hats should have some form of head band.

- Blocking should be smooth with any joins in felt work such as brims, and wiring (or bound wiring) done with concealed or neat even stitching.

- Fancy indented crown shapes should have been stiffened to maintain their shape.

- Hat bands should be neatly applied and finished.

- Linings should be applied from under the head band.

- The pile should have been raised and finished.

TECHNICAL – STITCHED HATS

- Seaming should be neatly sewn and well finished on all section joins.

- Brims and crowns should have suitable support, appropriately applied.

- Lining on washable hats must be compatible with other materials used.

FASCINATORS

- These may use any combination of decorative materials which are attached to a framework of suitable thickness.

- The framework may be made of covered wire or another suitable headband frame.

- The finished item should be lightweight, frivolous, and pleasing in appearance.

MODELLING

- Type of media should be suitable for the end use of artefact.

- Media should have been worked to produce a malleable consistency.

- Air bubbles should have been worked out and should not be visible.

- Surface indentation should be smooth, sharp, clear, and intentional.

- Surface colouring should have been appropriately applied/ used.

- Firing / heating/ drying should be done correctly to form a durable item.

- Glazing where used should have been applied to the whole – no omissions.

- Glazing should be of an even thickness – no runs or air bubbles.

- Glazing should have been done with clean applicator – no gritty areas.

- Finished artefact should be fit for purpose.

PARCHMENT WORK

- The design should be suitable for the type of materials.

- There should be no remaining traces of any guidelines used in marking out the design.

- Straight cut edges should be free from snags with even spacing if shaped.

- Deckle or serrated edges should be evenly worked.

- Pin holes should be evenly spaced throughout similar areas of the design and close enough to produce a lace effect.

- Embossed areas should be created with even pressure with line work of an even width.

- There should be no smudging at the edges of the embossing.

- Any colour should be applied to give a delicate appearance.

- The parchment should not show cracks, folds, or other indentations that do not form part of the design.

PATCHWORK

- Patchwork is done using new or recycled fabric. Whichever is used it should be in a good clean condition with no worn areas.

- Care should be given to the consideration of colour as forming a pattern throughout the item.

- Machined patchwork such as overlaid patches should be done with a suitable form of stitching which will either seal a raw edge or fix a neatly turned edge. The wrong side finish should suit the end use.

- Rectangular or triangular shape patches may be evenly attached by machine to form a regular pattern.

- Shapes with more than four sides will need to have been shaped over a suitable form so that the grain of the fabric is consistent throughout the item to prevent distortion during wear of cleaning. These will mostly need to be hand sewn together using inconspicuous small stitches.

- Fine fabrics will need to be lined with another this fabric to prevent turnings from showing through and spoiling the effect.

- Folded shapes should have been carefully cut to fit to their neighbours with no distortion.

- Edge to edge patches should be very carefully fitted with some form of backing fabric if flimsy or edged with a suitable coloured yarn and appropriate stitchery as in the case of suede or leather patches with a crochet edge.

- Applique shapes may be applied to the surface of some types of patchwork. These shapes should have been smoothly folded and neatly hemmed or top stitched in place.

PHOTOGRAPHY

General Schedule Classifications may be:

- Colour
- Digital black and white
- Sepia
- Dimension framework
- Mounted specification

Specific Group Classifications may be:

- Holiday snap
- Landscape
- Seascape or seaside study
- Architectural study
- Animal study

- Child study
- Amusing moment
- Action shot
- Mounted study
- Specific size

AREAS OF ASSESSMENT

GENERAL

- Dimensions should conform to statistics stipulated.

- Subject matter should be according to classification guidelines.

- Overall effect should be pleasing.

- Presentation or mounting should be appropriate and as stipulated.

- Appreciation of good colour composition and relative tonal values should be evident.

LIGHTING

- General lighting conditions should have been chosen to be appropriate to the subject matter.

- Flash reflection on reflective surfaces should have been anticipated and avoided unless for special effect.

- The position of photographer should have avoided self – shadows in the foreground.

- Precautions should have been taken to prevent or minimise red eye on portraits.

- The angle of light on the centre of interest should have been carefully chosen so that no undesirable areas of shadow are created.

LAYOUT

•	Positioning of subject matter should have avoided background interference.

•	Vertical objects should be shown as vertical.

•	The centre of interest should be in a suitable position to produce a well – balanced picture.

•	The dimensions of the centre of interest in relation to the background should have been chosen for maximum impact.

•	There should be no undesirable peripheral background included.

TECHNOLOGY –

•	Focusing should be sharp and clear on desired subject areas.

•	Close up work should have an appropriate depth of field.

- Shutter speed should have been chosen to prevent unintentional motion blur.

- Aperture and speed should have been chosen to prevent over/under exposure.

- Any enlargement should not be so great as to detract from clarity or resolution.

- White balance should have been suitably adjusted.

- Printing media should be appropriate to the type of subject.

POKER WORK

- The material chosen should be suitable for the type of work – usually wood or thick leather.

- The surface of the article should be well prepared and free of blemish.

- The design should be suitable for the work.

- Outline and trace marks should have been obliterated during the working of the design and should not be visible.

- Dot and line marks should show even graduations of colour.

- There should be no evidence of double marking.

- Added colour should be compatible and enhance rather than overpower the poker work.

- Added coloration should have been durably finished.

- The finished work should have been polished or glazed.

- The completed item should be suitably finished and presented.

- Any applied colouring or lettering should be translucent and compatible with the design.

- There should be no evidence of overburn.

- The finished article should be pleasing, clean and well presented.

POTTERY, CERAMICS, MODELLING AND DECORATION

Media used may include:

- Clay

- Clay with hardener

- Non – fired proprietary clays such as Das or Plastiroc plaster.

- Moulding powder

- Soft plastic modelling material

- Heat set plastic modelling material.

- Kiln fired materials.

ASSESSMENT

- Media should have been made sufficiently moist/malleable to produce a workable smooth slip.

- Media should have been worked to reduce risk of air bubbles and cracks in finished article.

- Any firing should have been done using correct temperature / time settings to produce a suitable degree of hardness for the material being used. There should be no evidence of over or under firing or heat setting.

- Any surface indentation should be sharp, clear and intentional.

- Applied colour should have been on dry surface to prevent colour bleeding using colouring material appropriate to media and be evenly applied.

- Glazing where used should have been applied to whole exterior with no omissions...

- Glazing where used should be thin (but may be several layers) having been thoroughly dried between layers to form a hard surface.

- Glazing should be of an even thickness with no runs or air bubbles.

- The glazing should have been put on with a clean applicator so that the surface is smooth and with no gritty areas.

THROWN POTS

- The shape should be evenly rounded on the exterior.

- The drawing up of the pot should have been done with an even pressure so that ridges are not formed on the outside or inside.

- The shape of the pot should be aligned vertically and not lean to one side.

- Any handles should have been evenly moulded and blended smoothly into the body of the pot.

- The handles should have sufficient strength to bear the weight of the pot and be firmly attached.

- Where there is more than one handle or protrusion of a similar nature, some form of symmetry of design should be evident.

MOULDED, MODELLED AND SCULPTED ARTICLES

- Smoothness of outline shape will denote knowledge of media being used and indicate the skill level of the user.

- Exterior surface should show uniform areas of texturing applicable to the design.

- The whole article should be well balanced.

- The base of the item should be such that it is stable when displayed on a flat surface.

CAST ITEMS

- Casting material should have been mixed so that the finished item does not flake of crack.

- The mixture should have been applied to the mould so that there are no gaps – an indication of the presence of air pockets.

- The design should be such that there are no fine protrusions which would break when removing the mould or during subsequent handling.

- The base should be sufficiently large/heavy to provide a stable support for the design.

- Excess moulding material should have been carefully removed from the outer edges of the base before finishing processes such as colour and glazing are done.

- Painting on china classes should have the painting done on commercially produced fine china with the decoration, glazing and firing the subjects of judgment.

PRESSED FLOWERS

- Materials used should have been fresh and in good condition.

- Materials should have been suitably thinned. prior to pressing.

- Pressing should have been done using sufficient weighting and absorption materials to prevent subsequent discoloration.

- Placement of materials when pressing should have been done to produce the best effect.

- Minimum overlapping or folding of leaves and petals should be evident as this produces thinner better – preserved results.

- Adhesives used for flat arrangements should not be visible.

- Any 'touch up' colouration should be imperceptible.

- The finished arrangement should be covered with a transparent sealing material to prevent damage or deterioration.

- The layout of an arrangement should be pleasing and well presented with good coloration and colour combinations.

QUILLING

- The type of material used to produce the quills should be of a suitable consistency.

- The quills should have been cleanly cut to an even width with no snagged edges.

- The scraping should have been done smoothly, so that there are no uneven bends or creases in the paper which will distort the finished effect.

- Coiling should be smooth and evenly graduated.

- Adhesive used for application to a surface should not be visible.

- Colouring applied to paper before cutting will result in a central band of white when cut and coiled. If this band has been coloured after coiling it should have been evenly and carefully applied so that it has not spoiled the side coloration of the quills.

- The finished design should be pleasing, well balanced with good colour effects and be suitable for the type of work.

- Presentation should have given consideration to the fragile nature of the work and be appropriate to the design.

QUILTING

- Care should be taken with the choice of wadding used to form the quilted effect. The end use should determine the weight, density, fabric composition and durability of the filling.

- All quilting stitches should be the same size throughout the item whether they are hand or machine worked.

- All-over patterning should be consistent and other patterns or highlights should be evenly distributed or well placed.

- There should be no accidental puckers or pleating in machined quilting.

- Italian quilting channels may be hand or machine worked using a double needle but should allow extra filling for movement on angles in the design.

- The backing fabric should be a suitable weight for the end use.

- Lining should have been used where appropriate.

- All sewing yarns should be of a suitable yarn composition for fabrics used.

- Edges should be neatly bound, piped, or otherwise finished.

- All corners are improved by mitring.

RAFFIA WORK

- Materials used may be natural or synthetic but should be in good condition and suitable for the end use.

- Woven work done over card should have sufficient spokes laid, which are evenly spaced.

- The edge should have been suitably bound separately to cover the remaining card.

- Coiled raffia work may be done using as a core either bunches of raffia strands of an even thickness or suitable string for strength.

- Coiled raffia work should be firmly fixed at the centre.

- The core should be an even thickness throughout.

- Weaving should have been done using evenly spaced stitches and wrappings.

- Articles with raised sides should be evenly raised and be of a symmetrical shape.

- Any attached handles should have been raised from the original core and should consist of sufficient rows to carry the weight of the article and intended contents.

- The core of the final row should have been neatly blended and finished.

RUGWORK

Methods of making floor coverings:

HOOKED

- This may be done using any form of yarn or strips of cut fabric fixed into a large weave fabric or firm weight canvas using a latch needle type hook.

- All strands of yarn should be knotted firmly to the base and the whole item should be worked in one direction.

- Each side of the backing fabric should be neatly hemmed and bound.

- The back of the base fabric should be lined with more pliable fabric to prevent excess wear on the surface fabric.

STITCHED

- The space between the rows of stitched yarns should be narrow enough to keep the pile of the surface reasonably upright.

- Finishing should be as for hooked rugs.

OTHER SUCH AS PLAITED AND POKED RUGS

- Strand of fabric or yarn used for plaiting or poking should be large enough to provide a decent thickness of rug or pile.

- Coiling should be firmly sewn together using a durable yarn.

- Seaming should not be visible from the upper surface with ends of the coils should be neatly finished.

- Poking should be done into a base with close enough weave to hold the yarn firmly.

- The depth of poking should be sufficiently deep. In all instance a backing fabric is preferable.

SALT DOUGH

- The dough should be even in texture.

- There should be no puffed areas indicative of wrong type of flour being used or too high an oven temperature.

- There should be no crumbling or cracking because of incorrect mixture.

- Dough should not be sticky from using too much water or oil in the mix.

- There should be no evidence of mould due to insufficient salt in the dough or dough not being properly dried out before shaping and decorating.

- The dough should be completely dried whether by oven, microwave or air.

- There should be some form of sealant used – PVA, other type of colourless thin glue or some type of varnish to prevent deterioration.

- Modelled shapes should be appropriate to the medium being used. Simple shapes are preferable.

- Any colouring should be applied after the sealant.

- Glitter and other embellishments should be firmly embedded within the dough and sealed securely in place.

SEA GRASS SEAT WEAVING

- This may be done with natural or synthetic yarn of suitable thickness strength for the task.

- The frame should have been suitably prepared and finished prior to weaving.

- There should be no spacing between the warp or weaving strands along the rails of the frame – only frame corners should be visible.

- Warp wrapping may pass over and under completely enclosing entire pair of rails or may be done with a back stitch on the underside or form the completed weaving in cross pattern.

- All joins in enclosed work should be done with a flat knot and on the inside of the underside of the work.

- Where it is not possible to hide the join, it should have been done as neatly as possible on the wrong side of the item.

- Coloured strands may be introduced but should have joins neatly hidden. Where it is not possible to hide the join, it should have been done as neatly as possible on the wrong side of the item.

- The tension of the finished weaving should be very firm.

SMOCKING

- The design and type of stitches should be chosen to suit the item being made and the position of the smocking on the item.

- Size between guide dots should be appropriate for design. On clothing items this is anything between 0.5mm and 12mm. The smaller the distance between guide dot, the more difficult it is to achieve even vertical folds.

- Gathers should have been evenly done and well placed in allocated vertical lines, drawn in to correct size and securely fastened.

- Decorative stitching should be even with rows kept to allotted lines.

- Gathering should have been removed after stitching has been worked and securely fastened.

- Evidence of dots should not be seen from outside and may be covered with lining on inside.

- Smocked panels should have been suitably seamed and finished when assembling the item.

- Machined smocking will have been done using a long stitch on the sewing machine, which as the stitches are quite small will not align as well as hand worked gathers.

- Decorative stitchery is done by machine or corded over these gathers.

- Smocked cushioning should be done using even folding and fastening on the inside with secure knotting.

- Piped edges for these are recommended.

- Circular smocked cushions should be neatly pleated front and back and the centre covered by a suitable or covered button.

SOFT TOY MAKING

- The schedule may stipulate which type of craft is to be used such as knitted, felt, fabric, fur fabric etc.

- It should be stipulated whether the toy is decorative or for child use. If the latter then all materials used should conform to relevant current BSI regulations.

- There should be no gaps in seaming or large stitches in knitting through which filling may be picked by little fingers.

- Filling should completely fill the toy so that it fills and holds its shape and should be of an appropriate type for the item.

- Filling should be evenly distributed and not lumpy.

- Any joints should be of the safety type and firmly fixed.

- Any other findings – eyes, noses, claws – must be of the safety type or neatly embroidered with all features evenly placed.

- Glass eyes may only be used on character toys which will not be used by children.

- Heads should be firmly attached and not weak and floppy.

- Toys for use by babies and toddlers should be washable or easy to hygienically maintain.

- There should be no puckering on seaming and corners and curves should have been snipped to give good shaping when filling.

- Any zips used should have shields to cover teeth and tags.

- All pins should have been removed.

- A toy is intended to give pleasure so the whole effect should be pleasing.

SPINNING

- End use of yarn is usually on attached label.

- Schedule, may stipulate, warp or weft yarn. Generally, warp yarn has a higher twist that a weft yarn.

- Ply should conform to the schedule and should be easily identifiable.

- Fibre content should be compatible with the same type of care.

- Synthetic and natural fibre content should be listed.

- Higher twist gives a smoother, stronger yarn and less hairy surface to finished fabric.

- Hank should be well wound and presented with 4 ties.

- The thickness of the yarn should be consistent throughout the skein except in unspun, tightly spun or slubbed areas in a decorative yarn.

TAILORING

- The schedule should state whether the class may include soft tailored as well as fully tailored items. These days most items are soft tailored for speed and convenience.

- Suitable fabrics should have been used appropriate to the craft and type of garment.

- Support fabrics weight, weave and fibre structure should be compatible with that of the garment fabric.

- Attachment by hand sewn or fusion methods should have fixed the support materials in the correct areas of use. Fusion methods should show no evidence of 'strike through.'

- There should be evidence of shrinking and taping as appropriate to produce the required degree of smooth contour on front edges and collars.

- Any dart shaping should have been smoothly done with bulk removed and well worked points.

- Pockets should have been worked using methods appropriate to the style and design with suitable reinforcement.

- Seaming should be smooth, well pressed, with bulk removed and with no impressions visible on the right side.

- Sleeve heads must be well shaped/smooth seaming and with appropriate support.

- Hems should be of an even width, well pressed, bulk removed and blind hemmed.

- Lining where fitted should have sufficient ease in length and width.

- Fastening should have been correctly and evenly positioned and neatly worked with even stitches and suitable reinforcement.

• The whole garment should have been well pressed before presentation but should not show signs of over pressing.

TATTING

- Yarn chosen should be strong enough for the type of work.

- Yarn thickness/type should be suitable for the design.

- Joins in yarn, should have been made neatly on the reverse of work.

- Ball and chain yarn should generally be of the same thickness / weight.

- Double stitches should be even throughout the work with no gaps.

- There should be no gaps between the rings and chains.

- Picots should be the same size throughout the work.

- The piece of work should have been blocked to shape for presentation.

- Edgings should have been mounted using a suitable method of attachment or other method of display.

UPHOLSTERY

The occasional item of upholstery is presented in the craft section of a local show. These are usually in the form of covered boxes, foot stools and drop - in chair seats.

- The frame used may be a purchased one, but credit is given for hand - made frames.

- Card or wood—corresponding sides of card or other material, which is to be covered should be identical.

- Covering should be done so that corners are mitred on the wrong side or are not visible when in place.

- Glue should be thinly but evenly applied with surface nicely smooth and not lumpy.

- Any machine seaming should be done using suitable yarn and stitch length so that seaming does not pull apart when being stretched into place.

- Webbing needs to be very well stitched and firmly fixed.

- Batting needs to be smooth and well covered.

- Folds made on corners of stools and seats should not be seen from the front of the item.

- All folding should be neatly done.

- The fabric should be tightly fitted with the warp grain of the fabric running from front to back and the weft grain from side to side.

- Stapling should be evenly done with no raw edges of fabric visible.

- Braiding should cover any tacks or staples and be firmly and evenly fixed.

- Any studs should be evenly placed and hammered to an even depth.

WEAVING

Weaving presented may be either in Loom, Braid or Card Loom form.

ASSESSMENT

- Warp and weft yarns should be compatible in fibre content, gauge and yarn structure.

- Selvedges should not show any distortion.

- Wales should be of an even width throughout.

- Passings should have been evenly beaten to produce a uniform thread count.

- Fancy weaves should be uniform throughout.

- Colour changes should have been neatly finished off.

- Warp relaxation should not be overpronounced.

- The face of the fabric should be the same throughout.

- There should be no distortion on the grains of the finished fabric.

- The finished work should be suitably presented and pleasing in effect.

WOODWORK: JOINED, TURNED AND CARVED

GENERAL

- The type of wood chosen should be appropriate to the task – hard or soft.

- All surfaces should have been smoothed before applying any texture.

- End grains should have been cut to avoid splitting along the grain.

- Glue sections should not show evidence of runs of surplus glue.

- Fine sanding should have been done prior to any applied finishing.

- Stain, wax or other colouring material should have been evenly applied with no evidence of runs or patchiness.

- The finished article should be stable with identical multiple limbs of an even length.

- Identical multiple limbs should all be set at a similar angle to their bases.

- Furniture surfaces should have been checked with a spirit level.

JOINED

- Joints should have been cut to fit perfectly to one another.

- Joint ends should have been smoothed before fitting together.

- Pinned joints should have been done with suitable nails, screws or dowels of an appropriate size and composition.

- Pinning should not have caused impressions of slippage of the tool used.

- The heads of any pinning should not stand proud but should have been recessed or levelled as appropriate.

- Any hinges, handles of other applied fixings should have been firmly and neatly fixed with recessing as appropriate.

TURNED

- Choice of wood should have avoided problem flaws such as knots with cracks.

- Turning should be smooth around the article.

- Ridges along the length due to uneven pressure should not be evident.

- Curves should be smooth in outline.

- Knops or other embellishments should be well shaped and spaced or grouped and clear in outline.

- The article should have been well sanded for maximum smoothness.

- Waxing and/or button polish should have been applied during turning.

- Any subsequent drilling marks should have been smoothed and finished to match the finish of the turned part.

- Face plate and jaw marks should have been removed and finished to match the finish of the turned part.

CARVED

- The wood chosen should be appropriate to the type of tooling to be done.

- Any background surface should have been prepared prior to carving.

- Tool marks should not be evident within the texture of the design.

- Relief carving should have sufficient depth to make the pattern of the design obvious.

- Outlines shapes should be well defined with clear sharp incisions if applicable.

- Untextured areas should have been suitably smoothed prior to finishing.

MARKING SCHEMES

There is no one correct way of marking handicraft items / classes.

POSSIBLE METHODS OF MARKING:

AWARD OUT OF A MAXIMUM

Selecting criteria and awarding a suitable mark out of a maximum for each criterion for each item and arriving at a total.

POSITIVE MARKING

Awarding a point for each positive achievement / skill evidence visible within each item and arriving at a total.

NEGATIVE MARKING

Deducting a point for each omission or incorrect area within the completed artefact.

ESTIMATION MARKING

Examining all items within a class then selecting by estimation the one demonstrating the highest skill / least number of flaws compared to other entries.

COMPARATIVE MARKING

All marking is done to compare one item against all others within its class, but you may find it helpful to devise a page / list of criteria with check boxes to use when judging difficult classes. These may be classes which contain more than one craft area. They may also include crafts with repetitive skills which take a long time to produce evenly or effectively.

COMPARATIVE JUDGING

- Factors to be considered for general assessment of all classifications.

- *Note. The longer the list of factors, the greater the degree of differentiation possible between exhibits of apparently equal merit.*

- Does the article presented conform to the class specifications?

- Are the materials used suitable for the design?

- Is the design and colour scheme pleasing?

- Does the exhibit achieve its aim?

- Was the article made using appropriate sequence of operations?

- Are the construction materials suitable for the design and end use?

- Are the construction methods suitable for the materials?

- Is any colouring suitably applied?

- Have appropriate finishing processes been correctly used?

- Has any embellishment been suitably applied?

- Is the whole exhibit well balanced?

- Is it a good example of its kind?

- What is the degree of skill required to produce the article?

- How many skills are required?

- How many different techniques have been used?

- Is the article indicative of knowledge of advanced techniques used to advantage?

- Is the product superior or excellent in any way from its competitors?

HANDICRAFT JUDGING FOOTNOTES

- The time taken to judge each item will be longer than for judging horticulture as there is much more to be taken into consideration.

- There are many different skill areas to take into consideration as well as the variety of materials, tools and types of items produced.

- Each item within any one class will often require at least 3 minutes to adequately examine its construction and degree of excellence.

- A similar amount of time will be required to determine which of the various first prize winners merit the award of any cups or shields.

- Large shows with lots of entries will require more than one judge.

- Kits where used should be stated unless the class is specifically for kits and cannot be given as high an award as an originally designed item of an otherwise similar standard.

- Articles presented should be as stated in the schedule and should be clean and not have any sharp objects present.

- Modern technology enables modern methods to be used.

- Different types of **judges' qualifications and methods** means that marking schemes and methods will vary considerably.

- All judging should be based on what is **good practice** within any one craft discipline whether new or traditional methods are used.

FINALLY

Difference between judging craft and produce:

- There is no **NATURAL** element in craft production – everything is a matter of **CHOICE** and **LEVEL OF SKILL**.

- The **GOOD JUDGE** should know what those skills are.

- There is **NO 'ONE POINTS'** system which covers everything – i.e., all crafts.

- There is **NO 'ONE CORRECT'** way of making anything.

- There is **NO 'ONE CORRECT'** way of judging/ marking anything.

GLOSSARY

Randing – weaving in and out of the upright stakes of a basket formation to form a firm shape.

Scalloming – tying pliable stakes over a firmer rod to form the neat upper edge of a basketry item.

Trank – the single piece of leather which forms the front and back of a glove without the thumb, fourchettes and quirks.

Thonging – very thin long strip of leather which is used to sew pieces of leather together in place of spun sewing yarn. It may also be used to form a sewn edging using a decorative stitch.

Selvedges – the edges at the sides of a woven piece of fabric which prevents fraying. The selvedges are in the direction of the warp grain of the fabric. Frequently done using a plain weave and more tightly woven so that the edges in less secure types of weave (such as satin or herringbone) can be stabilised as weaving takes place. Often hooks or claws are used commercially to keep the fabric stretched taut during any surface or other processing. When the claws are removed, there may be some relaxation shrinkage.

Marmie Vergo Certificate of Education, LCGI Creative Crafts.

Marmie Vergo began her career as a science teacher and in 1970 qualified in City and Guilds Advanced Fashion and Creative Crafts. She worked as a part time lecturer in these subjects and was later appointed as Head of Sector a position she held until 1998. She joined the Ann Ladbury Lecture Service, giving freelance lectures to women's groups throughout the West Country from 1974 onwards and did embroidery work which was used in the Ann Ladbury BBC television programmes and books and briefly acted as a technical consultant promoting Panda Ribbons. She has regularly been a handicraft judge at Horticultural Society, Townswomen's Guild and Women's Institute shows as well as being an External Verifier for City and Guilds from the 1970's until 1999 at various colleges in the Southwest of England. She has recently been the Chairperson of the Dorset Federation of Horticultural Societies Guild of Show Judges and has devised courses for the training of handicraft judges.

www.ingramcontent.com/pod-product-compliance
Lightning Source LLC
Chambersburg PA
CBHW041143110526
44590CB00027B/4107